SWANSONG 𝄞 SC

by Rosemary

PART ONE - SWANSONG

Edited by Johnathon Clifford
of the National Poetry
Foundation
0329 822218

Gills Verse Publications
11 Lupin Works, Worcester Road,
Kidderminster, Worc's, England.
DY 10 1JR

Printed by Sales Print Design Ltd

©Rosemary Arthur 1989 and 1992

This publication is protected by Copyright. No part may be reproduced without the prior permission of the Author.

British Library Cataloguing-in-Publication Data.

*To all dear and loyal friends
and to my mentor, Jonathon Clifford
of the National Poetry Foundation*

Several of these poems have been previously published in my book
'The Gift of Imagination' - 1988.

Previous publications by the same author:

Aspects of Autumn (1984) ISBN 0 946204 51 9
Miscellany (1985 & 1988) ISBN 0 86303 229 -X
The Halcyon Days (1985 & 1989) ISBN 0 86303 324 -5
The Gift of Imagination (1988) ISBN 0 9511898 2 4
The Gift of Imagination Illustrated (1992) ISBN 0 9511898 9 1
Swan Song (1989) ISBN 1870556 75 5

ISBN 1 897641 00 1

Contents

PART ONE

Page:

4	Touchstone
5	Sea Calling
6	Another Cleopatra
7	In Retrospect
8	Brief Interlude
9	A Private Celebration
10	The Masterpeice
11	One Grief Too Many
12	Transplant Reject
13	No Connection
14	Forbidden
15	The Masquerade
16	Bed Time
17	Distant Father
18	Mint Sauce
19	Echoes Of The Sixties
20	Re-think
21	A Rooted Stone
22	In Search Of Ravens
23	French Perfume
24	Love Story
25	Peony Pavan
26	The Blooming Of The Gorse
27	Question Master
28	Corn Dolly
29	Flashback
30	The Wide Brimmed Hat
31	Big Spender
32	Enhanced By Sadness
33	If He Should Go
34	One Way Street
35	The Vigil
36	The Shadows On The Path
37	The Happy Prisoner
38	Swan Song

TOUCHSTONE

One sad November day when everything around was grey
the sky, the air, my mood,
I gave myself a new name
returning to my roots and memory.
Arthur was my Father's name and in his home
he was a king
his word was law, he dominated everything:
he had no time for sentiment, and kept his kind heart
well concealed in tears of helpless laughter;
I often think of him, remembering what he used to say;
his influence is almost tangible.

Mother was Rose by name and Rose by nature
softly curved and sweet scented,
the family revolved around her
even the house lamented silently if she was away
no longer warm and comforting like her cooking -
her pastry was as light as thistledown.

My namesake was Aunt Mary, a widow of a Yorkshire miner,
fate dealt her a paltry hand and she had
few luxuries to compensate, but she had other riches
and found consolation in her children and
her imagination.

I felt reborn returning to my roots
and childhood memory rattling its bones,
stepping stones that lead to greater understanding.

SEA CALLING

From this landlocked Midland shire
I feel a great desire to smell and taste the sea
to watch once more the waves break on the shore,
drink deeply of the salty air
and walk barefoot in the shallows.
A yearning reflected in the sad ebb tide
takes my heartache in its lap
sucking out the pain of grieving.

The house is empty now
I hear no sound of distant voices
all doors open on to nothingness:
my thoughts imprison me with memories
of how it used to be.

I shall sit in loneliness until the waves
roll in again - creep nearer, ever nearer,
cleansing and levelling the sand
softening the sharp edges of my pain,
and its relentless advance I know
will slowly give me back again
my failing courage.

ANOTHER CLEOPATRA

She was not young, and certainly no beauty:
her charismatic radiance made the supermarket a stage;
the seried ranks of beans and tuna fish, her chorus;
the shoppers a restless, changing audience
as people looked, then looked again, trying in vain
to define the mystery of female scorcery.

Old men gazed with wistful memory, turning away,
envious of youth and fulfilled dreams -
the young men, hope still burning
stared with timeless desire
eager as impatient dogs, waiting for a sign
to chase and retrieve the thrown stick.

From a distance the women watched
wary of the eternal Eve;
ready to spit with venom-tongue,
green demon's claws unsheath.

Concious of her power but feigning unconcern,
an enigmatic smile upon her face,
she moved with sensuous grace -
another Cleopatra.

IN RETROSPECT

I regret the years between
if only we could have been wise beyond our youth;
we were inseparable as all young creatures,
growing into love;
playing in the endless sunlit days
emotions soaring pavilions high
hit by a dancing blade of laughter;
finding wonder in an uncharted land
of pounding drums in wild cacophony
breaking the fragile shell of innocence;
we briefly held the flowers of paradise
in our careless hands,
blossoms that withered before they bore the fruit,
for youth needs to spread its wings to new horizons;
to tread the distant alien soil
and taste the wine on other lips.

The drums are muffled now, the heartstrings muted;
in retrospect I feel we have been truly blessed
to have grown from the wonderous awakening of youth
into the maturity of fulfilment;
the ageing barren tree still feels the sun and rain;
sap rises in the eternal spring
and emerald transforms the hazel eye;
the errant key turns in the lock,
two parts combine to form the perfect whole;
and once more we share the bread and wine of life.

Your arms enfold me close in bonds of love;
tender as the dawnlight, blind as the mole;
the velvet light is soft and warm;
the lamp of love is lit and bright;
why should I grieve for years now gone
for you and I once more are one.

BRIEF INTERLUDE

If only I could hold you in my arms,
keep your image in my eyes,
share again your laughing banter
we would make the heavens ring.

I sit before the fire and
listen for your step along the path,
the lifting of the latch;
but I do not feel alone, your presence fills the room
tangible as the firelight -
comforting as a glass of wine.

How I long for you -
the sound of you, the touch of you,
the scent of your skin -
a bowl of peaches fills my mind with thoughts of you
and the bloom softening your cheek;
as I drink deeply of the juice
I remember your voice caressing words you spoke
as they caressed my heart
and shaped me to your pleasure
clay beneath your fingertips
until I called a truce.

My life began the day you looked into my eyes
and ended the day that you last smiled;
when you are here with me once more
we will make heaven sing.

A PRIVATE CELEBRATION

Entering the church to see
her young friend wed
was a testing time for her,
a kind of watershed
with memories of her own marriage,
her wedding day, warm and bright with hope
so slow to fade but
finally betrayed.

Back in her quiet room
she kicked off her shoes and
sank into a chair, relieved that
little guilt remained, for there had been
no need to wait for death's release;
she was happy to be free
and other arms would gladly
make him welcome.

She filled a glass with wine,
smiled in pure elation, and
drank a silent toast to freedom -
a very private celebration.

THE MASTERPIECE

They told me the picture was by an impressionist;
it certainly made an impression on me;
colours all blurred and indistinct,
like the world looks to me after a night
when wine flows too freely
and I awake with someone else's head.

I think I could paint a picture one day
if I had a canvas and some paint
and my head stopped throbbing;
why not use the walls in Lucinda's room?
they look so bare with all the posters gone -
it could encircle them like Monet's waterlilies.

I feel sure it will be a masterpiece -
I'll start right away;
I'll go out and buy the brushes and some paint
when my head stops throbbing
and my hands stop shaking;
maybe not today,
perhaps tomorrow,
or the day after.

ONE GRIEF TOO MANY

My father died alone
slipped out of life without me there
I must not make the same mistake again
let someone die before they see
compassion in my eyes, and love.

He was no easy man to know,
strong in body and inventive mind
so many thought him stern and cold but
he could be kind and gentle
with animals and to me
with a twinkle in his eye he would
often let me try to twist him round
my little finger.

I still feel his presence near;
I hear him chide me if I am foolish;
I look for his smile of pleasure
if I use knowledge he had dearly bought
but freely gave to me;
I miss him more as I grow old,
my shadow becomes his shadow;
passing time bring no consolation
his death is still my deprivation.

TRANSPLANT REJECT

It seemed a good idea to find a smaller place
neat and modern, labour-saving -
this house is all of that, but clinical
and cold, not where I could grow old gracefully
everything is so impersonal - no lived in atmosphere -
I feel it almost an offence to cough.

Our old house had its faults
but welcomed me with loving arms
and whispered to me softly through the landing window.
I miss the walk through tangled grass to stones
where Tibby, Mr Pusskin and old Hector lie
half forgotten with the growing pains of childhood.
We did not need the attic any more
but hopefully in time to come there will be
another generation filling it with toys
or so they might have done if we had stayed.
Here there is no room for sentiment.

I have not transplanted very well
my roots are bruised and torn and I am alien
in this too perfect sterile place.
I miss the slipshod corners and the daisies on the lawn
and shall become quite stunted without spontaneous joy.
no wild flowering.
The soil and everything around is antiseptic, but
I shall struggle to survive, although I need
a slightly decadent touch before I'll ever bloom again.

NO CONNECTION

How fickle is a woman's intuition -
she felt the time was right,
that he would not want to waste another night
and leave her all alone -
it made her pick up the phone to dial
the number that came so naturally
as familiar as her own name;
she listened to it ring with bated breath.

His voice was just the same, sexy with a hint of promise -
until she spoke
then ice crept into the words and almost broke her heart
cold and distant as the Arctic sea.

With a few brief words he'd gone, out of her life
and there would not be another reconciliation;
just one ring would last for ever
it's diamond facet caught the light
and winked in consolation.

FORBIDDEN

I often dream of meringues, eclairs and crepe suzette,
gateaux, ice-cream sundaes, chocolate;
treacle tarts and apple turnovers,
light souffles and sweet pavlovas;
stomach drooling, eyes devouring,
the mere temptation's overpowering -
who devised we should be ruled
by calories not luscious food?

Once more we start a slimming craze,
chicken salads but no mayonnaise;
brown rice like dessicated bones
ensure we are sylphlike clones;
lettuce, cucumber and tomatoes,
apples, grapes and avocados -
colourful as a still life painting,
and as unexciting.

We can feast our eyes but not our body,
keep thoughts pure and celibate,
by turning desire into negation
and only rarely celebrate;
deny temptation in the name of sweetness
and all things taken to excess -
they are as the fruits of Eden;
objects of desire,
but quite forbidden.

THE MASQUERADE

He had an extra chromosome, the magic some folk have
that makes a man seem head and shoulders high
in everything but stature
and all would sit enthralled at his voice
melodious as an Aeolian harp,
strings plucked by silvered words
would set the wheels of imagination turning
and put a face to many a woman's erotic dreams
as other actors seemed dwarfed, measured
against the yardstick of his talent.

He did not need a theatre, he would perform
in any place and create a scene
his words and gestures recalling roles that won acclaim,
but everything was just one size too large
for so cramped a stage as he would erupt
and spume as Etna's flow, and in their unease
all would slowly drift away.

In melancholy he would turn to the arms of nameless women
with no pretence of love, or seek
blissful oblivion in the golden malt
and dream of endless curtain calls.
Few who saw him on the stage knew of the terror
in his heart - beneath the mask of confidence
crouched the inner man, sad and lonely
dreading advancing age when he would be forced
to abdicate the theatrical throne that was his world.
Envied for his fame and image of success
he lacked true friendship
he had received most honours but there will be
no Oscar for the finest performance of his life,
the role he portrayed of a happy man;
a courageous masquerade.

BED TIME

When our hearts were young and bodies willing
bed was more for loving
as years go by and blood is cooling
bed is more for sleeping;
now everything has changed once more
we draw the curtains, close the door and
we are in another world - we dine
with a flask of wine, and sandwiches
or crusty bread and cheese, or if he agrees
a creamy naughty from the patisserie.

Then warm and close beneath the duvet
we are happy, feeling groovy,
enchanted by the midnight movie
the bed is once again inviting,
infinitely more exciting,
in future I shall not be seeking
another bed for only sleeping
for bed is made for loving, laughing, teasing,
everything that we find pleasing
and of course, eventually sleeping.

DISTANT FATHER

He missed her sleepy, out-of-focus morning face,
the upturned nose, and
the questing toes seeking warmth behind his knees;
he missed the life they'd shared for a decade -
her cooking and her company,
the laughter and the temper
quick to flare and quick to fade
and most of all
he missed the children.

He missed the daily contact, the little things -
walking with the dog in quiet leafy woods,
joining in the laughter at Grandpa's tales,
and the treat that never fails -
burgers at MacDonalds.

His sons were growing up without his
loving, watchful eye,
he now had to stand by and see
a stranger, not of their blood, their genes
their parentage
guide them through their teens, be there
at every stage;
hear as their childish voices soar and dip
teach them to shave soft down on upper lip
whilst he stood aside, growing more distant
a little farther every year.

MINT SAUCE

Each Spring I think of him
and the way he would call me 'Baa-Lamb' -
such a silly name -
he would say "we all love a frisky little lamb"
and my reply, always the same, was
"Especially with mint sauce", and he would laugh and say
"Not yet, you are far too young today".

I wonder if I would know him now? It was so long ago;
he was tall because my hair got all caught up
on his waistcoat buttons when he held me close to him
but the memory of his face is rather dim
the blue may have faded from his eyes
and the russet hair will have greyed
but I can still see his hands, gentle loving hands
with thumbs curved right back in a boneless arc
like Cupid's bow, and I can remember
the sweet scent of the soft grass in the top meadow.

He may not know me now I am no longer frisky as a lamb
but I would say, "do you think I'm ready for the
mint sauce now?" And hopefully he would laugh
and remember the way it used to be.

ECHOES OF THE SIXTIES

No one called him inarticulate
he always spoke his mind
in words not always kind but straight to the point
until it came to love;
undemonstrative he said he was, and that was true
but love was there
tongue-tied and self conscious;
he never told me he would liked to have a child
until it was too late
wrapped in my content I was not aware of this,
his   need - I only wanted *him*.

He would send his love to me via Nat King Cole
and that says it all
for Nat died over twenty years ago
but still travels with me on journeys in the Eighties
when I am quite alone, an empty seat beside me.
There might have been a child here with me now
if he had told me of his love all those years ago
instead of a growing longing in my head
and a warm brown voice singing in my ears.

RE-THINK

I used to think -
to go to bed and sleep
without the finger of conscience
prodding me awake
was worth a hundred hours of
wanton pleasure, but
a halo is uncomfortable to wear
when it grows tighter every year
and the days drag by
on leaden feet.

Maybe just a few hours of pleasure
would only warrant a gentle shake
and then
I could go back to sleep
warm and smiling -
reminiscing.

A ROOTED STONE

We watched him play the field
a handsome, well-heeled Romeo
and the girls would come and go
as varied as the flowers in May.

Their names would fascinate
Fiona, Isabelle and Kate,
Felicity and Zoe, Annabelle and Chloe,
till there was Clare
with her rare gift of tranquillity;
she looked at him with cool green eyes
and he was hooked.

Her serenity and simple charm was a calm
haven
in his stressful thrusting world
they were as one
as necessary to each other as roots locked
around a stone in bone-dry ground
impregnable, indestructable.

IN SEARCH OF RAVENS

Last year two ravens circled in the sky
the sombre hills echoed their cry confirming
a vast loneliness with only sheep and their lambs
as witness.

One who saw the ravens in their ritual courtship dance
marvelled at the unexpected chance
to see them swooping, diving, twisting, turning
time and time again
flying upside down like acrobatic planes
in a spectacular feathered air display;
large birds using the wind like animated kites
powered not by thrusting jets
but fast beating wings in fierce duet.

Two young lovers went to seek the ravens
and on the highest peak it seemed
the world was at their feet
and love made it a retreat from wordly cares;
they embraced and then
all thoughts of ravens were forgotten.

FRENCH PERFUME

When I was young the image of the District Nurse
was someone capable and strong
who tended the very young and very old
but now she is from a different mould
and no longer smells of Dettol.

I watched her gentle hands tend him intimately,
impersonally
and as she bent low to smooth his pillow
he smiled faintly and seemed content.

I caught a trace of perfume as she passed;
she saw surprise on my face for then I realised
why he had stirred in reminiscent memory;
she laughed and said, "I often contrive
to show them they are still alive
by giving them a whiff of 'Poison'
and they love it!"

LOVE STORY

I know he loves me:
it must be true,
he tells me every day
he wants to spend his life with me.
He has such fantasies of how perfect life would be
together
just the two of us, we need no other
or so he says.

He loves to look at me, to listen to my voice,
to touch me,
watch me sleep.
He hates to tear himself away, to leave me,
wants to be with me for always,
or so he says -

His love will last for ever and grows day by day
but has never felt this way before
but did he not say he would
love *her* "for as long as he shall live"
and if he was with me each day
there would be no more mystery;
love is wayward, unpredictable,
how can I say if this desire will last
I may grow tired of him.

PEONY PAVAN

Rich crimson petals stain the path
as glorious in dying as in brief blooming
when the hot sultry breath of June
sucks the silky flowers dry until
they spill frail as tissue paper, all too soon.

Each years holds the promise that the peony
will grace and dominate the border for a longer time,
the large leather-leaves open like extended hands
begging for reprieve in a voiceless plea
as summer wind and weather quickly ends
their spell of splendour,

The long awaited blooms return again each year
but fail to stay for any time at all
only sadness remains as blood red stains fall
upon the stones to mark their passing.

THE BLOOMING OF THE GORSE

In Spring the birds will mate, the sap will rise
and men will gaze with lustful eyes
at girls whose thoughts are often filled
with dreams of bridal gowns, instinct instilled
when the voice of the turtle can be heard
nesting is not only for the birds
love follows neither rhyme nor reason
Cupid's arrows have no season.

Country folk say kissing's out of fashion
when the gorse is out of bloom,
but with no end to love and passion
they are very wise, for of course
even in the bleakest winter
there are flowers on the gorse.

QUESTION MASTER

He was only four, well four and a half actually,
very important that half -
and tackled life like a rugby forward
leaving behind a narrow trail of havoc.
One day he said, "I miss my Gran, she took me to the park;
are there ducks on the pond in heaven Grandad,
and roundabouts and ice-cream? -
She always bought me ice-cream".

He found sad relics in the cupboard in the hall
"this is Buster's ball and lead, isn't it Grandad
and his basket - where will he sleep now;
did he go to heaven in a rocket and
how did they know which way to go
did Jesus leave a light on in the porch;
will Buster be able to talk now he's in heaven
and say he likes sugar in his tea at night,
and go for long walks with Jesus?
Your face looks funny Grandad,
have you got a pain in your tummy?
I'm hungry, let's go and see what Mummy's got for tea
I'd like 'battled' fingers and beans -
don't look so sad, Grandad, I know Buster's dead
but I'll go for walks with you instead
you'll like that, won't you Grandad?"

CORN DOLLY

When corn is green it stands strong and stiff
as soldiers in a vast battalion
regimented by wind and rain swaying in unison
to command of an unseen sergeant
breathing instructions to bow to every wind that
blows.

When corn is gold it is less disciplined
mellowed by warm sunny days
ears filled with the hum of
satiated bees, relaxed,
receptive to many a bright temptress
who flaunts her scarlet petticoats
and flirts with wide open eyes
living for a wild brief day
she is wanton in her choice of bedfellow
with an open invitation to dally awhile
before sharp blades mingle the petals with the grain
or roll them in the hay
like the bold camp followers of old
exuberance is all too brief
for the poppy from the lane.

FLASHBACK

Yesterday I looked at a child and saw my sister's face
the clear grey eyes and laughing mouth -
one crooked tooth raising the upper lip
in the familiar fascinating slightly crooked smile
and I was transported back some twenty years.

The hair was not the same at all, short like a boy,
not thick and dark swinging to the waist in heavy plaits.
I would have traded everything to change
my fair and wispy curls for that
great glorious mane of hair,
but there is no envy left in me now
for I am still alive.

Today I looked at the girl again
and saw no similarity
she is no pale shadow, no mere facsimile,
the fleeting impression is gone for ever.
But just for one brief moment there was no doubt
that she was my sister's child.

THE WIDE BRIMMED HAT

Floating gently on the early morning sunlit tide
like a small deserted island abandoned by its owner
was a wide brimmed hat
forlorn and forsaken by the one who'd worn it
a sad reminder of the futility, the inevitability of it.

The children looked for her each day
a solitary woman sitting in the café
the cup of coffee by her side, cold and untasted.
Her face had a faded slowly dying look
as if some thing had sucked away all life
leaving an empty shell.
Her eyes shaded by the brim, stared out to sea,
she was just killing time.

It will remain a mystery, a haunting memory
of a lonely woman sitting in a cafe,
the epitome of tragic isolation that
wore a wide brimmed hat.

BIG SPENDER - BLACK COUNTRY HUMOUR

What kind of crisps d'you want, he'd say
or would you like a Mars, or a Kit - Kat?
and I'd settle for that
it's not the food I go for
but the conversation.

Sometimes we go into the country
it's lovely there, the air
is so different;
and when money's a bit short, you have to sort-of
be careful;
one day we went to Talybont, in Wales you know -
in October when prices were low -
and he had a big steak and I had
poached salmon and salad -
we went mad that day, he says we may
go back some time, but it was only two years ago
and we mustn't make a habit of it;
perhaps when we're old we'll have more meals like that
'cos I've been told
there's nothing else to do then, is there?

It's not that he's really mean
just a bit more keen on the things
that don't cost money -
so we often take a snack, and it's great
when it's sunny, but we always take a mac.

I think I'll cut a dash today,
spend some of my cash
have a Shandy with the crisps
and dream of Talybont.

ENHANCED BY SADNESS

The haunting sound of a solitary harp;
the clear notes of a clarinet;
the refrain of a familiar tune we can't forget -
a predatory eagle hanging like a kite;
the plaintive fox cry in the night;
a well-worn empty chair -
all have the unmistakable feeling
of sadness and despair.

So it is with a woman's face;
after sorrow comes a certain grace;
defenceless with her trembling lips,
pale listless hands, cold fingertips;
seeking an unknown way with pain filled eyes
as sorrow transforms and glorifies.

There is a special stillness
and an air of hidden strength
disguising naked truth;
a heart laid bare.

IF HE SHOULD GO

If he should go, try not to grieve too long
nor beg him stay, for that would be wrong -
we cannot hold a man against his will
be he a husband, lover or a child -
so tell your heart it should be still
for anger and bitterness will hurt no one but you
not him, nor her, nor anyone, but you.

Cry your tears in oceans if you need
but cry when you're alone
find a loving trusting friend to listen
pour your heart out to her
but never moan
look at the world with eyes that hide no shame
make others wonder why he left
and think he was a fool who played a silly game.

Just let him go
for if you hold him back by threat or guilt
what have you got?
A man, or just an empty shell?
no joy in that for you, or him
no thoughts to share, no words of comfort
just a life of Hell -
so let him go
he may come back again.

ONE WAY STREET

I am bone tired:
the journey from my country lanes
has been too long:
I ache for respite from the noisy streets:
too many mechanised chess pieces
on a tarmacaddamed board:
powered horses in their starting stalls
that jostle for position
strain on the green:
rear on the red:
tearing nerves and rubber
to painful shreds.

I turn into a one-way street:
slow down, nervously wondering:
dreading:
uncertain of the end, I hesitate:
but there is no other way,
no turning back:
despite my loitering
the one way street comes to an end.

THE VIGIL

What shall I do when you are gone
no longer here to share?
You who are my restricted world,
my life and my despair -
all passion spent, all dreams are dead
just barren thoughts to fill my head.

I watch you as you sleep and reminisce
of the first *'hello'* , the first shy kiss,
but now I see a body but no soul
the passing years demand a heavy toll,
and everything must wait
for death may strike too soon or drag too late
as the burden grows more heavy
and patience wears more thin through endless nights,
watching dawn begin.

Sometime I long to be myself and get away
but how shall I feel when I am freed
from the vigil fate decreed?

How many years to wait, how many tears to shed?
I fear what lies ahead
before the dual carriageway becomes a single track
and as a weary traveller
I seek solace
looking back.

THE SHADOWS ON THE PATH

Paths are not always bathed in sunlight
or enhanced by moonlight
we are grateful for the shadows
when the sun is riding high and
the sun is far too hot from a clear blue sky,
but when the night is drawing near
they grow menacing and stark
with fingers stretching out across the path
moonlight makes pools of blackness
mysterious and dark, forming shadows on the ground,
silently they gather, making not a sound.

There are nights when nothing stirs
everything is still, just the shadows moving
and the air is chill
it is as though they wait for something
certain it will come to pass -
haunting images in a darkening glass -
so they stay, patient sentinels of fate
no need to hurry to that special date
time alone will show what lies before us, good or bad
and if it should be sad
in the dawn of sorrow's aftermath
we come to realise the meaning
of the shadows on the path.

THE HAPPY PRISONER

You hold me in your arms
yet I feel free
for this is where I long to be
locked in our private haven
night merges into day
however it is begged to stay -
my horizon is the distance of your smile
and your laughing eyes that so beguile
have captured me these many years
so happily.
So keep me safe within the bonds that hold me fast
the bonds of love - long may they last -
for there is no escape for me
with no desire to be set free,
this enclosed world wherein I lie
is one I need until I die.
I am content to be your happy prisoner
and hope to stay like this for ever
- come what may.

SWAN SONG

I tell myself I shall not fall in love again
let someone take my heart, wring it out
and peg it on the line to dry like some old
rubbing rag:

I will not be at someone's beck and call
but be myself, to do as I please
not rush to pleasure others like a fawning dog;
I will be *strong and resolute,*
know my own mind - say what I think -
just for the hell of it!

With no one there to tug the reins
life may be dull
or boring - if so
I shall buy myself a hat and
find a ring to throw it in
or tilt it at a saucy angle to intrigue;
I might dance barefoot in the meadow grass
one bright shining morning, magically young in
my wild brief swan song,
or I will borrow Grandma's bonnet
and go looking for a windmill.

I think this may be <u>my</u> 'Swansong' but my friends
laugh in disbeleif - we shall just have to wait and see.

PART TWO

SOLO VERSES and OBSERVATIONS

This Section was not edited by
The National Poetry Foundation -
once more I am a free spirit
and on my own.

Page:
- **41** Poetry Is
- **42** Pen Portraits - (1) SILVIA
- **43** Pen Portraits - (2) MAIRI, MAIRI.
- **44** The Church of St. James, 1992.
- **45** Another Eden
- **46** Armchair Traveller
- **47** Another Wide Brimmed Hat
- **48** Lost Journey
- **49** Vacant Possession
- **50** The Bird of Sorrow
- **51** Refurbishment
- **52** Who is Counting?
- **53** Letter To The Chronicle
- **54** The Bridge
- **55** Listen

August 1992.

POETRY IS

Poetry is a healer
a revealer,
emotion's inner voice;
longings in a soundless printed cry
sorrow translated;
dreams expressed.

The yearning,
the heartbreak pouring out in creation
whose birth pangs fade into
words on a printed page.

Hope is the seedcorn
words flowing,
an everlasting harvest growing;
experiencing a deep exhileration -

Poetry was my salvation.

"Poetry is a silken thread, my own hands weaving"
                                            John Keats.

PEN PORTRAITS - (1)

SILVIA

To me she was my dearest friend,
colourful, well-rounded and full of joy
and as welcome as a Summer afternoon,
familiar as a well-loved tune,
and as refreshing as cucumber sandwiches for tea
under the cedar tree.

To her children she was like Autumn,
mellow and warm, she could transform
chaos to calm, and her loving arms
would shelter them from impending harm.

To him, viewed through a lover's eyes
she was ageless - he looked at her
with rose-tinted tenderness and
the years disappeared into memories of the days
when she bewitched him in so many ways;
her laugh, as sparkling as fountain water
and her gentle smile,
her loyalty and style
had filled his heart with love
and he was bonded still.

Who is Silvia? what is she
that all her swains commend her?
Holy, fair and wise is she
the heaven such grace did lend her
that she might admired be.   William Shakespeare.

PEN PORTRAITS - (2)

MAIRI, MAIRI

Often quite contrary -
her garden grows profusely, nothing is sedate
as green fingers plant and cultivate
the flowers into a living tapestry
completely unrestrained, completely out of order
spilling over paths and borders, all
seeding, blooming where they fall.

Mairi is elusive, fey -
an enigma, here today and gone tomorrow -
an unknown quantity like an iceberg
three parts hidden, deep and cool,
the one part visable warm as waves on a shallow pool
lit by Summer sun.

A one man woman,
desired by many kept at bay
a full arm's length away.

Days of youthful joy and shining eyes
deny the passing years as though they have never been,
with lips curving in a laughing mouth
she could still be sweet sixteen
as laughter tugs at the heartstrings
giving a glimpse of what might have been.

THE CHURCH OF St. JAMES - 1992

The church had intrigued me for over twenty years
standing solitary on a lonely hill;
from afar it looked neglected,
unloved, desolate;
so I always resisted the temptation
to drive down the narrow lane
to take a closer look, but the other day
I did just that.

The lane curved under the shelter of the hill,
winding steeply to the top
and in a clearing stood the church
beside a quiet pool with wild ducks
paddling contentedly among the reeds
and the surrounding trees and shrubs
bending low over the water.

A long dead tree, sturdy as a giant but
blasted by long forgotten lightening
and bleached by endless Summers, stood sentinel
making this a magical place, tranquil and serene.
Three partridges scurried through the adjacent field
the only sign of life in this typical English scene;
no sound but the song of the birds.

The church door was locked;
I could not see inside, but read the notice
on the board in the little porch, it read
"The Church was built in 1625
Services are held every Sunday
but due to vandalism last year when
the organ was stolen, the Church will remain locked"
How times have changed
this picture of the peaceful countryside
belied the truth
that today nothing is inviolate.

Church of St. James, Arrow & Weethley.
Alcester.

ANOTHER EDEN

No serpent lurks beneath the tree
entreating me
to pick the fruit and tempt the man -
for no apples grow within my garden.

Women today are emancipated
more sophisticated
not slaves to men as they were then,
and we learn there is a subtler way
to help improve their knowledge.

Some things never change
but appetites both new and strange
can lure and tantalise -
temptation in a new disguise -
as apples are no longer cute
we can choose a sharper, slightly bitter fruit
which covered with a rich short crust
inspires desire and we know we must
still feed the inner man, and
it is surprising what you can do if you try
with damson tart or gooseberry pie
or even lots and lots
of tender apricots.

ARMCHAIR TRAVELLER

How wonderful it is to travel
see strange and beautiful places,
inaccessable years ago - just names on a page.

When I was young I longed to see the world;
I dreamed of sunlit vistas,
of bright blue oceans lapping golden sands,
of peaceful lakes, and happy, smiling children.

I longed to see the wonder of Africa
the fascination of India,
the wildness of Nepal,
the enigma of China,
the isolation of Alaska,
the legend and mistique of South America,
the grandeur of Canada and
the vastness of Russia.

But I did not know of the misery of flies,
and bugs that bite
of heat and smells and sickness,
of long delays at airports struggling with
the baggage and fractious, screaming children,
the drunken hooligans, and the hassle over
foreign currency and language, but

Yesterday I visited ten countries, relaxed
and comfortable in my easy chair,
free from heat and cold and stress,
and joy of joys, escorted by Alan Whicker,
I was quite content - filled with happiness, - I'm told
I must be growing old !!!

ANOTHER WIDE BRIMMED HAT

The hat in the centre of the window
drew her eyes as some alluring magnet;
A pale cream straw with a soft pink bow
around the flat wide brim;
the perfect hat to wear on her wedding day
to match her rose bouquet -
a ridiculous extravagance -
a hat to be admired, but also
a hat to make her a bride to be desired.

She dreamed of the day, and pictured the way
she would lift her face for his embrace,
but the brim was far too wide
for him to hold her tight
and that would not be right,
so then she knew for her wedding she would wear
a single rosebud in her hair
fixed to a velvet band
then he could hold her close
for she had come to understand
that only someone seeking isolation
would choose a wide brimmed hat.

LOST JOURNEY

Every journey has to start from somewhere
travelling unromantically from A to B,
journeys with diversions or
confrontations with reality.

The quiet country lane,
meandering vaguely as an ancient stream
uncertain of its destination
like some half forgotten dream.

Narrow lanes can change to dual carriageways,
straight and wide and fast
with no time to dally on the way
all links severed from the past
with hedges trimmed into conformity
by mechanical precision, and we forget when
they were tended by the hands of patient men.

Time has lost its meaning at the ending of a lease
as ghostly generations tend the farms
attracting towndwellers
to imagined peace.

VACANT POSSESSION

I have repossessed the room: in theory at least.
His photograph looks at me from the wall and
40 years of memories fade and all is silent.
The room is still, quiet as the grave;
death had come with stealth, pausing to give false hope,
standing in the wings to take a prolonged curtain call
which came when all were weary and emotion kept on hold
for so long, finally dissolved,
sorrow mixed with blessed relief.

After he had gone, I rushed into a flurry
of activity, turning out all drawers and cupboards
until there was no trace of who had lain there
watching the days come and go;
I changed the curtains and the carpet
and the wallpaper so that the room became
a different place, no bed or bedside table
but a study where I could sit and write -
or at least that was the plan.

But now it is as though I have obliterated
his presence; thrown out 40 years
as I had wished to throw away the years
of pain and suffering, but now
I feel I have swept away the other years
of happiness and sharing.

When I go into the tidy soul-less room
I feel I have changed it all too soon
and discarded his personality with the rest,
gone from all but photographs and memories.

The other day I drove to the little church
where we were married so many years ago,
and there on the board were letters in gold
HERE IS FORGIVENESS AND WITH FORGIVENESS, PEACE
my heart was lighter as I slowly drove away,
the words were there for all to see;
I felt they were meant just for me.

After many years of illness, my husband died in August 1990.

THE BIRD OF SORROW

I call your name and the wind snatches it away
I cry and the sun dries the tears that fall
I run aimlessly around and the rocks cut my feet
I sleep but dreams elude me
I listen for your voice but silence taunts me
My eyes are dimmed by endless searching
for the face that haunts me
My hands are tired from soundless praying
My arms are empty as my heart.
My mind is dead, thoughts leading nowhere
as the seasons come and go so slowly
to pass me by unheeding.

I must release the bird of sorrow
send it winging on its way
Pick up my courage, hug it tightly
look forward to a brighter day.

Chinese proverb:

*"You cannot stop the bird of sorrow
from flying over your head
but you can prevent it
from nesting in your hair."*

REFURBISHMENT

My kitchen window faces North and is always cool
and as I stand at the sink I dream
I can see a quiet stream
with weeping willows swaying to a gentle breeze
as they lift their skirts and run away
like shy maidens in the days gone by
but when in reality I saw the dull grey roofs nearby
I felt hemmed in and sad
until I had
a great idea.

Now I am re-born
for my kitchen is filled with poppies
and golden ears of corn;
what a transformation can be created
from a few rolls of wallpaper
and imagination.

WHO IS COUNTING?

There was a time when I would say nonchalantly
"But that was before the War"
and folk would nod in mutual remembrance
when I spoke of childhood memories, but
now in the 1990's I stop in mid sentence
and only mention the 1930's with other
greyhaired contempories
for younger folk would look at me with surprise
and think "before the War", count up to fifty
and no doubt say to themselves
"she must be ancient"!

So now I have learnt my lesson
and always hesitate before I say the fatal words
"before the War", and
try to keep an agile mind
and hope that folk will be kind
and think I am not so old after all.

LETTER TO THE CHRONICLE

To the Editor,

I went for a walk the other day
and passed the fountain in the Park -
it was painted yellow, blue and red -
I shouted at some youths but they
just laughed and said
"When the sun shone the fountain looked
just like a rainbow, so when the Council
turned it off, we painted one instead,
it looks better that way"
I can't understand the youngsters of today
disgraceful I call it.

And another thing,
my dog cut his foot on a Coca-Cola tin
when he was performing on the playing fields -
the children of today have no discipline
they shouldn't throw litter on the grass
but put it in the bin;
they should be taught to be clean and tidy
or should be banned from The Green;
we must get our priorities right,
I shall still take my dog to The Park,
I've trained him not to bite
and only bark at strangers.

I had to make my protest and get it off my chest,
but finally I must say I think
this country is on the brink
of going to the dogs.

Signed: Open-minded. Colonel, (Rtd).
           Datchet.

THE BRIDGE

Look at me and I shall see
all that is precious to me,
in the twinkle of an eye there will be
wonder, there will be honesty, there will be joy,
friendship, laughter, love.

Through the archway of the years
the span of thirty years is crossed
just by a smile, and hands reach out and intertwine
as though the years between have never been;
memories flood back of happy days;
the bridge is in the mind
but strong and indestructible
if love is there.

LISTEN

Listen to the wind, sighing in the trees,
rustling the leaves, dancing in the breeze.
Listen to the sea, rippling on the sand,
rushing to the shore, crashing on the land.
Listen to the rain, chattering on the roof,
gurgling with noisy mirth,
before splashing on the barren earth
to flow inevitably down to the restless sea.

Listen to the birds, singing in the trees
free as air,
listen to them in their golden cages
safe and dry,
chirping happily,
but forgetting how to fly.

Listen to the voices, crying in the wilderness,
strangers to every kind of happiness,
lend an ear to their sorrows and their fears,
lend a shoulder for their tears.

Listen to your own heart beating
to the rhythm of the age,
listen to your heart's pounding
in a tight ribbed hollow cage;
listen to your heart's whispering
begging you to listen to the voice of wisdom
guiding from above,
and listen, always listen
to the voice of love.